2 —

Yellowstone
NATIONAL PARK

*The World's First
National Park*

Photographers – Carr Clifton, Chuck Summers, Dai Hirota, David Muench, Dennis Flaherty, Dick Dietrich, Erwin & Peggy Bauer, Howie Garber, © Jeff Foot / Larry Ulrich Stock Photography, Jeff Gnass, Jerry Mercier, Jerry Pavia, John P. George, Jon Gnass, Larry Ulrich, Marc Muench, Michael Loomis, Richard Cummins, Richard Strange, Robert Winslow, Russ Finley, Scott T. Smith, © Scott T. Smith / DanitaDelimont.com, Stephen Trimble, Tess Young / Tom Stack Assoc., Tim Fitzharris, & © William Neill / Larry Ulrich Stock Photography

ISBN: 978-1-60068-086-1

Second Printing, February 2008

www.impactphotographics.com
4961 Windplay Drive, El Dorado Hills, CA 95762

Printed in China

Abyss Pool, West Thumb Geyser Basin

One of Yellowstone's most spectacular hot springs, Abyss Pool is located in the West Thumb Geyser Basin area of the park. It is one of the deepest springs in the park measuring 53 feet in depth, and varies in color from turquoise blue to emerald green to various shades of brown.

Firehole Falls

Firehole Falls is a 40 foot waterfall located on the Firehole River south of Madison Junction. The name seemed to have been applied during the 1890's, but was recorded by A.C. Pearl and F. H. Bradely in 1871.

Kepler Cascades

Kepler Cascades were named by Kepler Hoyt, the twelve-year-old son of the then-governor of Wyoming, John Hoyt. These 100 to 150 foot waterfalls are on the Firehole River above Old Faithful.

Tower Falls

Tower Falls is located on the northern loop of Yellowstone National Park between Canyon Junction and Tower Junction. Fed by Tower Creek, it plummets 132 feet and eventually enters into the Yellowstone River.

Gibbon Falls

Gibbon Falls was named in 1871 by W.H Jackson and John M Coulter. This 84-foot waterfall tumbles over remnants of the Yellowstone Caldera Rim. The rock wall on the opposite side of the road from the waterfall is the inner rim of the Caldera.

Old Faithful & Old Faithful Inn

Old Faithful erupts more frequently than any of the big geysers, although it is not the largest or most regular geyser in the park.
Its average interval between eruptions is about 91 minutes, varying from 65 - 92 minutes. It was named for its consistent performance
by members of the Washburn Expedition in 1870.

Old Faithful Inn

The Old Faithful Inn was designed by R.C Reamer of Seattle, Washington who was a mere 29 years old at the time. His goal was to incorporate the natural beauty of the park, and thus a lot of natural stone and woods were used in his design. One of the most treasured features of the hotel is the 80-foot chimney, which hosts eight fireplaces and contains 500 tons of hand-quarried lava rock.

Old Faithful

Old Faithful Geyser was named in 1870 by surveyor General H. D. Washburn. Its eruption height varies from 106 to 184 feet, its eruption intervals vary from 45 to 92 minutes. The temperature before eruption is 240°F, and during the eruption some 3,700 to 8,400 gallons of water are discharged.

Lion Geyser Group, Upper Geyser Basin

The Lion Group consists of four geysers: Lion, Lioness, Big Cub, and Little Cub, which are all connected underground. Of these, Lion (seen here erupting in the background) has the largest cone and eruptions. Eruptions of Lion Geyser last 1 - 7 minutes and are often preceded by sudden gushes of steam and a deep roaring sound, hence the name Lion.

Sawmill Geyser, Upper Geyser Basin
Sawmill Geyser features highly variable eruptions lasting anywhere from nine minutes to over four hours, with a typical interval of one to three hours between eruptions. It received its name because of how the water spins in its crater during eruption, resembling the rotating blades of a circular saw.

Grand Geyser

An eruption of Grand Geyser, the tallest predictable geyser in the world, occurs every 7 - 15 hours. A classic fountain geyser, Grand erupts from a large pool with powerful bursts rather than a steady column like Old Faithful. An average eruption lasts 9 - 12 minutes and consists of 1 - 4 bursts, sometimes reaching 200 feet (60m).

Grotto Geyser

Grotto Geyser erupts about every eight hours, splashing to a height of 10 feet for 1 1/2 to more than 10 hours. The odd-shaped cone that gives this geyser its name may have resulted from geyserite covering the trunks of the trees that once grew there.

Riverside Geyser, Firehole River

Riverside Geyser erupts at seven-hour intervals to a height of 75 feet for a 20-minute duration. It has a temperature of 201.2°F with a column of water shooting at a 70° angle over the Firehole River.

Morning Glory Pool

Morning Glory Pool is one of the most popular springs in the Upper Geyser Basin. Though only one natural eruption in 1944 has been recorded, the pool is still considered a geyser as evidenced by the runoff channels leading to the Firehole River. The pool was named after the morning glory flower because of its brilliance, which has now diminished due to the drop of water temperature.

Sapphire Pool

Between 1883 and 1886, geologists Walter Reed and Arnold Hague named Sapphire Pool because of "the color of its water". Geologist Hague thought that it was the finest hot pool in the Park.

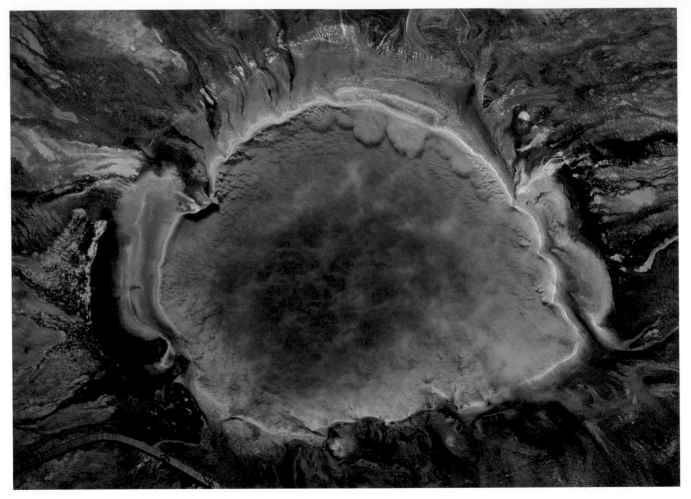

Grand Prismatic Spring, Midway Geyser Basin

Midway Geyser Basin is seen here from the air. Grand Prismatic Spring, in the center, has the distinction of being the earliest described Yellowstone thermal feature. It is the largest hot spring in the park with a diameter of 370 feet.

Firehole River, Midway Geyser Basin
Firehole River received its name from early trappers in the area who believed the steam rising from thermal vents was smoke from underground fires and commonly referred to the small mountain valleys as a "hole". The river is fed by hot water from the Upper, Middle, and Lower Geyser Basins which can raise the temperature by 18 – 47 degrees F.

Fly Fishing
Fishing has been a major visitor activity for well over a century. Due to this history, fishing continues to be allowed and can complement, and in some cases even enhance, the park's primary purpose to preserve natural environments and native species.

Clepsydra Geyser

Clepsydra Geyser is located in the Fountain Group of the Lower Geyser Basin. Its name is Greek for water clock, and was given because the geyser used to erupt regularly every three minutes. Since the 1959 Hebgen earthquake, however, Clepsydra erupts almost without pause.

Great Fountain Geyser

The sun setting over Great Fountain Geyser is just one of the many spectacular views at Yellowstone National Park. Located in the Fountain Group in Lower Geyser Basin, it is one of the Park's premier geysers, erupting in 75 to 200 foot fountain-type displays.

Hot Spring near Great Fountain Geyser, Lower Geyser Basin
Many visitors are surprised to learn certain algae and other organisms can live and grow in hot springs. In a very general way, the hotter the water is, the lighter the colors (cream to yellow). The cooler the water is, the darker the colors (green).

Tangled Creek, Lower Geyser Basin

Tangled Creek travels through the south side of the Lower Geyser Basin where it eventually joins up with the Firehole River. It received its name in 1885 by the USGS because of the network of separate channels that cross and re-cross each other.

Gray Wolf *(Canis lupus)*
The gray wolf mates for life and lives in packs of family members and relatives. The strongest male is the leader of the pack and all the members help to care for the young. Known for its howl, the various whines, yelps, growls, and barks help to keep the pack together. A lone wolf will give a beautiful and haunting howl when separated from its pack.

Grizzly Bear Cubs *(Ursus arctos)*
Grizzly cubs are exceptionally small and weigh only about one pound at birth. As they grow they begin to venture out of the den on their own, but remain close to their mothers and siblings for several years. Bear cubs have much to learn about survival from their mothers before they can become independent.

Bison *(Bison bison)*
Bison refers to the North American species as opposed to bovids in other parts of the world, which are called buffalo. Bison are related to domestic cattle, sheep, and goats. They stand 5 ½ feet high at the shoulders, and adult males (bulls) weigh 1,200-2,000 pounds while females (cows) weigh 700-900 pounds.

Steamboat Geyser, Norris Geyser Basin

Norris Geyser Basin has been flowing for more than 115,00 years and contains the world's tallest active geyser, Steamboat. Measurements from a scientific drill hole have produced a temperature of 459°F only 1,087 feet below the surface, making this the hottest geyser on the continent.

Norris Geyser Basin

Norris Geyser Basin is the oldest and hottest thermal area in Yellowstone National Park. It is one of the most diverse and unpredictable areas in the world with the highest recorded temperature of any thermal site. The area was named after Yellowstone's second superintendent, Philetus W. Norris, who was also responsible for constructing the first roads to the Park's major attractions.

Main Terrace, Mammoth Hot Springs

Travertine Terraces are seen at Mammoth Hot Springs in the northwest corner of Yellowstone National Park, Wyoming. Travertine is a form of calcium carbonate that is dissolved from limestone beneath the ground, and is then carried to the surface by hot water. The colors represent a variety of bacterial algae that survive at various water temperatures.

Yellowstone Bus

2007 marked the long-awaited "homecoming" of eight vintage White Motor Company buses to Yellowstone for in-park tours! The returning fleet includes two 1936 vehicles, four from 1937, and two from 1938. These buses were originally used as part of a large Yellowstone fleet that numbered in the hundreds.

Mammoth Hot Springs

Mammoth Hot Springs are the main attraction of the Mammoth District, which is also home to the Park's Headquarters. These travertine formations are quite different from the thermal areas elsewhere in the park. As hot water rises through the limestone, large quantities of rock are dissolved by the hot water, and a white chalky mineral is deposited on the surface resulting in the formations seen here.

The Roosevelt Arch

The Roosevelt Arch stands at the north entrance of Yellowstone National Park. At the time of the arch's construction, President Theodore Roosevelt was visiting the park. He consequently placed the cornerstone for the arch, which then took his name and was dedicated in 1903.

Bunsen Peak

Bunsen Peak and the "Bunsen Burner" were both named for the German physicist, Robert Wilhelm Bunsen. It stands 8,564 feet high (2,612 meters) and may be climbed via a trail that starts at the Golden Gate. The peak is also interesting because it was ravished by fires in the 1880's and then again in 1988.

Cow Moose & Calf *(Alces alces)*

Moose, the largest members of the deer family, breed from early September to November and one to three calves are born in May or June. Calves weigh 25 to 35 pounds at birth but grow rapidly; adult females (cows) weigh up to 800 pounds and males (bulls) up to 1300 pounds.

Petrified Forest, Specimen Ridge

Specimen Ridge, located along the Northeast Entrance Road east of Tower Junction, contains the largest concentration of petrified trees in the world. Specimen Ridge provides a superb "window" into the distant past when plant communities and climatic conditions were much different than today.

Yellowstone River

The Yellowstone River begins on the slopes of Yount Peak, south of the park, and travels more than 600 miles where it empties into the Missouri River in North Dakota. It is the longest un-dammed river in the lower 48 states and is a popular spot for fly-fishing.

Upper Falls *(inset)*, **Lower Yellowstone Falls**

The falls are erosional features formed by the Yellowstone River as it flows over progressively softer, less resistant rock. The Upper Falls is upstream of the Lower Falls and is 109 ft. high. The Lower Falls is the highest waterfall in the park, standing at 308 feet high and is often described as being more than twice the size of Niagara.

Grand Canyon

The Grand Canyon of the Yellowstone is a very recent geologic feature at no more then 10,000 to 14,000 years old. It is roughly 20 miles long, starting from the Upper Falls and ending in the Tower Falls area, and is 800 to 1,200 feet deep and 1,500 to 4,000 feet wide.

Elk *(Cervus elaphus)*

Elk are members of the deer family, with mature males or bulls weighing from 600 to 900 pounds. Bull elks' massive antlers are shed in late winter or early spring every year.

Pronghorn *(Antilocapra americana)*

The pronghorn antelope is more at home in open fields and sagebrush than any wooded area. Hence, he is most often viewed in the northern part of Yellowstone. Easily the fastest animal in the park, the antelope has been timed at speeds of 60 m.p.h.

Bighorn sheep *(Ovis canadenis)*

The Bighorn Sheep is a good swimmer and excellent rock climber and jumper. It has hooves that are hard at the outer edge and spongy in the center that provide good traction on sheer rock.

Hayden Valley

The Hayden Valley was once filled by an arm of the Yellowstone Lake. Due to heavy sediments left by the lake, water cannot percolate readily into the ground creating the marshy area that we see today. This area is one of the best places in the park to view animal and bird life.

Fishing Bridge

The original fishing bridge was built in 1902, and was later replaced with the current bridge which was completed in 1937. This was historically a tremendously popular place to fish, due to the fact that it was a major spawning area for cutthroat trout. However, the bridge was closed to fishing in 1973 because of the decline of the cutthroat population. Since that time, it has become a popular place to observe fish.

Lake Yellowstone Hotel

Located on the Yellowstone Lake, the Yellowstone Hotel opened its door to guests in 1891. At that time it was not a particularly distinct looking hotel, however massive renovations that occurred through the 1920's created the gracious landmark we see today. The Hotel was placed on the National Register of Historic Places in 1991 and remains one of the oldest and largest wooden structured hotels in the United States.

Fishing Cone, Yellowstone Lake

Fishing Cone is one of the most famous thermal features in Yellowstone National Park. This cone-shaped hot spring was first observed and documented by the Washburn Expedition in 1870 as party members watched a fisherman's trout accidentally fall off the hook into the hot spring; when the fish surfaced it was literally boiled.